SEEKING TRUTH

Devotion vs Spirituality

A Study Guide to the Word of God

DENISE D. SNOW

WESTBOW
PRESS®
A DIVISION OF THOMAS NELSON
& ZONDERVAN

WestBow Press books may be ordered through booksellers or by contacting:

WestBow Press
A Division of Thomas Nelson & Zondervan
1663 Liberty Drive
Bloomington, IN 47403
www.westbowpress.com
1 (866) 928-1240

ISBN: 978-1-5127-2845-3 (sc)
ISBN: 978-1-5127-2846-0 (e)

Library of Congress Control Number: 2016901148

Print information available on the last page.

WestBow Press rev. date: 4/26/2016

INTRODUCTION

Throughout the study guide, readers will see the acronym RTB. It stands for, "Read the Bible," and it is a reminder to hold onto God's words. Reading the Bible will bring major breakthroughs to a person's life. Use this guide as a tool to demonstrate how. The apostle writes in 2 John 10–11 that if anyone comes to you bringing a message that is *not* the doctrine of Christ, *don't* receive it and *don't* encourage it! The passage goes on to say that if you do, you are participating in evil. Mark 7:13 states that when one is stuck in tradition, then God's Word has no effect. Some churches and religious groups have blinded people from seeing God's true love by distorting God's Word. Throughout this multiple-choice, self-help, question-and-answer study guide, you will discover, without re- course to traditional religious views, the shocking truths about what God has really said in His Word. You must take the first step and read the Scriptures yourself. Use this study guide as a reminder to RTB and not hold on to past religious views. As you do, divinely revealed knowledge and answers will arise from these pages by God's will alone.

Paul reminds us, "But if our gospel be hid, it is hid to them that are lost: In whom the god of this world hath blinded the minds" (2 Corinthians 4:3–5).Why do people act like they can't understand the Bible on their own? Eileen Caddy, spiritual teacher, once said,

> I would never say that hearing this voice within, as I hear it, is the only way of experiencing God. It isn't, because everybody has a different way. That's just my way of doing it. God is within everyone, *"Do you not realize that you have within you all wisdom, all knowledge, all understanding? You do not have to seek it without, but you have to take time to be still and to go deep within to find it. Many souls are too lazy or feel that there is so much to be done that they have no time to be still and go into the silence. They prefer to live on someone else's wisdom and knowledge instead of receiving it direct from the source themselves."[1]*

Proof that God will reveal truth, wisdom, and knowledge to an individual can be read in Matthew's gospel.

> He saith unto them, But whom say ye that I am? And Simon Peter answered and said, Thou art the Christ, the Son of the living God. And Jesus answered and said unto him, Blessed art thou, Simon Bar-jona: for flesh and blood hath not revealed it unto thee, but my Father which is in heaven. And I say also unto thee, that thou art Peter, and upon this rock I will build my church; and the gates of hell shall not prevail against it (Matthew 16:15–18).

---

[1] http://seekeronline.info/journals/y2006/mar06part2.html

God has built the church on revealed knowledge by God and those who believe in Christ, the Son of the living God. According to 2 Corinthians 4:3–5, the gospel of Jesus Christ is hidden to those who are lost, who believe not because their minds have been blinded by other influences. The meaning of lost is to be led astray. Jesus never built a brick-and-mortar church. The church, the assembly, which Jesus Christ built, was a body of believers who believed he is the Son of the living God, and the gates of hell cannot prevail or triumph against us.

Read Luke 4:16–20 Jesus went into the synagogue, the assembly, opened the Bible, and read the plan and purpose for his life and then sat down! Notice he read the Bible literally. Jesus spoke of those in the synagogue as hypocrites and heathens in (Matthew 6:2 and 6:7). He went onto say they have their reward. Jesus said he had come to preach deliverance to the captives. The meaning of captive is to be taken away or contained. Jesus restored belief in the things of God, revealing God's truth instead of the lies of other influences!

Individuals should ask themselves two questions: 1) What church or religious organization do I belong to? 2) Am I being blinded, contained or influenced by their traditions? Too often churched and unchurched folks go through life being convicted and accepting struggles as the will of God for their life because of their lack of God's truth about who they are in Christ Jesus. When people don't allow God to work through them, knowingly or blinded, their struggles are great!

Jesus said he came to set us free, to deliver us from bondage and oppression. It wasn't the act of sin but disobedience, not hearkening to the voice of God, which put bondage, the curse, and the resulting struggle on Adam and mankind, according to (Genesis 3:17). Sin is just that—a missing of the mark according to Jesus in (John 8:3–12). In Matthew 16:17–18 Simon Bar-jona was blessed and empowered because he heard the voice of God. God wants direct communication with us as he did with Adam and Eve. The recommendation was for man to always pray, to meditate in the Word day and night, and to observe to do what is written. In doing so, we receive not the spirit of the world but the Spirit which is of God, understanding the things freely given to us of God (1 Corinthians 2:12–13).

Seeking Truth: Devotion vs. Spirituality The Study Guide to the Word of God was designed to get people to be still and to go deep within themselves. It develops the reader's comprehension skills by causing him or her to think on the passage that was read by presenting a question. The Bible was inspired by God according to 2 Timothy 3:15–16. It is God's words! It is a publication for the way unto salvation. Salvation is the power and ability to be adopted as a son of the Most High God. How people should live is answered in Deuteronomy 8:3 they shall not live by bread alone, but by every word that proceedeth out of the mouth of the Lord.

Individuals should not allow the traditions and religious views of today's churches to deceive them. There is a need for a deeper revelation of the Bible, the word behind the Word, as some of today's pastors and religious leaders would have one believe, but it should come from God and not them (Jeremiah 1:4–9). God meant what He said when He said it! RTB! In Matthew 24:35 Jesus said, "Heaven and earth shall pass away, but my words shall not pass away." Isaiah 55:11 says, "So shall my word be that goeth forth out of my mouth: it shall not return unto me void, but it shall accomplish that which I please, and it shall prosper *in the thing* whereto I sent it."

Father, I pray that all eyes that read the pages of this guide and your Word will be opened to the things of God (2 Kings 6:12–17).

In Jesus name, Amen

Instructions: Read the passage and answer the question based off of what you read in the Bible. Do not answer questions based on previous knowledge. Read the "Note" or "Think" section and the reference Scripture before moving to next question.

1. In the beginning, God created the following: A) The sun and the moon B) The land and the sea C) The heavens and the earth D) None of the above *Genesis 1:1*	2. In six days God spoke all things into existence. What did He create? A) Earth, heavens, land, and water B) Daytime, nighttime, sun, and moon C) A man, plants, animals, and fish D) All of the above *Genesis 1:1–31*	3. What was the first form of life God created? A) Man B) Plants C) Animals D) Fish *Genesis 1:20*
4. In whose image was man created? A) In the image of an animal B) In the image and likeness of God C) In the image of a fish D) None of the above *Genesis 1:27*	5. What is God? A) A man B) A spirit C) A man and a spirit D) None of the above *Genesis 1.2*	**Note** Genesis 1:26 states, "God said, Let *us* make man in our image, after our likeness." The *Us* is the Father, the Word, and the Holy Ghost, and they are one. Refer to 1 John 5:7.
6. What was man made of at the time of creation? A) Flesh B) Spirit C) Both A and B D) None of the above *Genesis 1:26*	7. Who created the spiritual man in Genesis 1:26? A) God B) The Word C) The Holy Spirit D) All of the above	8. God gave the spiritual being— man—total control or dominion over what? A) Over the fish of the sea B) Over the fowl of the air C) Over the cattle D) Over all the earth and over every creeping thing that creepeth upon the earth *Genesis 1:26*

9. What gender did God create man?

A) Male
B) Female
C) Both male and female
D) None of the above

R T B

Keep studying!

Genesis 1:27

---

10. What did God tell the spiritual beings, them, to do?

A) Be blessed
B) Be fruitful and multiply
C) Replenish and have dominion over the earth
D) All of the above

Genesis 1:28

Note

Genesis 1:28 states, "And God blessed, empowered them to multiply the earth and have dominion on and over it" (spiritual beings on earth having babies).

R T B

---

11. How many days did it take for God to create all that He had made?

A) Five days
B) Six days
C) Seven days
D) None of the above

Genesis 1:31

---

12. What did God do on the seventh day after days of creation?

A) He walked the earth to view His creation.
B) He rested and blessed that day.
C) He made angels to watch over man.
D) All of the above

Genesis 2:2–3

Note

Let there be no confusion over whether days were twenty-four hours long or something else. Read these Scriptures:

Genesis 1:5
Genesis 1:8
Genesis 1:13
Genesis 1:19
Genesis 1:23
Genesis 1:31

R T B

---

13. After God finished the heavens and the earth, who was there?

A) Adam
B) Eve
C) The host
D) None of the above

Genesis 2:1

Note

Genesis 1:26 refers to God creating man in His image and likeness, and in Genesis 2:1 man is referred to as *host*. Earlier translations translate the term as *heavenly host* or *angelic beings*.

R T B

Keep studying!

Note

In Genesis 2:2–4, notice the change from God to Lord God. Remember that God rested from all *He* did in Genesis 2:2. Also remember in Genesis 1:26 the U*s* is Father, Word, and Holy Ghost, and they are one. Ponder on the roles of God the Father and Lord God the Son. Study John 1:1 and John 1:14. Jesus acknowledged he is Lord God in Matthew 7:22–23.

R T B

Think

Read Genesis 2:4–5 carefully.

Q. What has to happen before a plant or herb can grow or produce?

A. First, it must be planted in the ground as a seed; second, it must be watered.

Now read Genesis 2:5 again.

Think

Genesis 2:6

Q. Why was a man needed to till the ground if the man created in His image and likeness was already there in Genesis 1:26?

A. According to Genesis 3:22, they were two different species.

RTB
Keep studying!

14. The man formed in Genesis 2:7 was formed from what?

A) The dust of the ground
B) From an ape
C) He evolved from a caveman.
D) None of the above

Genesis 2:7

Note

Tradition has taught that the man in Genesis 1:26 was placed inside the man in Genesis 2:7. If that were the case, man would have already known good and evil when tempted by the Serpent in Genesis 3:4–5. Remember in Genesis 1:26 man was created in God's image and after His likeness.

Note

This may bring enlightenment to those who have been taught that the man in Genesis 1:26 and the man created in Genesis 2:7 are one and the same. This may also bring enlightenment to those who have questioned why everything was spoken in Genesis 1 and then starting in Genesis 2 things were formed or created. God the Father rested, and Lord God, the Word, is still working.

15. What role was God functioning in when the man from the dust of the ground was formed?

A) As God the Father
B) As God the Holy Ghost
C) As Lord God the Word
D) All of the above

Genesis 2:7

16. The man created from the ground became what?

A) A speaking spirit
B) Like God and in His image and likeness
C) A living soul
D) Jesus

Genesis 2:7

Note

The man created in Genesis 1:26 and spoken of as host in Genesis 2:1 was created in God's image and likeness; he is a spiritual man. The physical man spoken of in Genesis 2:7 is a living soul. Soul equals the brain, which equals the mind, will, and emotions, and the living cells— flesh and blood.

RTB
Keep studying!

Note

Further confirmation and enlightenment of these two different beings roaming around on earth at the same time will come over the course of studying Genesis.

17. Where did Lord God put the physical man?

A) On the earth
B) To the east of the garden of Eden
C) Both A and B
D) None of the above

Genesis 2:8

18. What was man's responsibility in the garden?

A) To do as he pleased
B) To reproduce
C) To dress it and to keep it, to work the grounds
D) To make it home

Genesis 2:15

Note

A command was given to tend, guard, and keep the earth. Why would this be necessary if man was the only one there?

19. According to the Bible, who had dominion over the earth after the physical man was created?

A) Spiritual man, host
B) Physical man
C) Both A and B
D) Adam

Genesis 1:26

20. What gender did Lord God give the man from the dust of the ground, physical man?

A) Male
B) Female
C) Both male and female
D) None

Genesis 2:15

Note

Notice in Genesis 1:27 the genders male and female were mentioned during the man's creation, and the term *them* is used.

Notice in Genesis 2:7, which talks about the man formed from the dust of the ground, gender is not mentioned. But it does imply singular form with the words *his nostrils*. Later this is followed up with the creation of woman.

21. Lord God told the physical man he could eat from every tree in the garden of Eden but one. What was the name of that tree?

A) The Tree of the Knowledge of Good and Evil
B) The Tree of Death
C) The Tree of Life
D) All of the above

Genesis 2:16–17

22. What did God say would happen to man if he ate from the Tree of the Knowledge of Good and Evil?

A) He would know good and evil.
B) He would be like God.
C) He would die.
D) All of the above

Genesis 2:17

23. What did Lord God call the physical man from the dust of the ground?

A) Adam
B) Son
C) Man
D) Eden

Genesis 2:19

24. Who named all the plants, trees, and animals?

A) God
B) Adam
C) Eve
D) All of the above

Genesis 2:19–20

25. How did the Lord God form a woman?

A) From the dust of the ground
B) From an ape
C) From the rib of Adam
D) None of the above

Genesis 2:21–23

26. Lord God's purpose for creating the woman was to give Adam companionship, a wife. How does Lord God view this union?

A) It's not very good.
B) It's okay for now.
C) They shall be "one flesh" (as one).
D) None of the above

Genesis 2:24–25

Note

Notice the spiritual man was not a suitable mate. Remember Genesis 1:28 states, "And God blessed," empowered them to multiply the earth. Lord God did not give the physical man any commands to be fruitful, multiply, or replenish the earth at the time he was created or when woman was created to be a help mate

27. In the garden of Eden, what crafty and deceitful creature convinced the woman that by eating from the Tree of the Knowledge of Good and Evil she would become "wise like gods"?

A) A lion
B) A serpent
C) A owl
D) None of the above

Genesis 3:1-6

Note

Refer to Revelation 12:9 to support that the serpent is Satan, and the Devil, which is the Evil One.

Note

Notice in Genesis 3 the serpent caused the woman to doubt God's Word by saying, "Ye shall not surely die."
Q. Why should the woman believe the Serpent?
A. In Genesis 3:3 the Serpent was wiser than all the beast of the field.

Research the biblical definition and use of the term *beast* and review Genesis 1:28. Also note in Genesis 3:6 the reason Eve ate the fruit was to become wise.

28. What did Satan do to the woman's mind and thought process when he questioned Lord God and intentionally mislead her about what Lord God said? He caused the following:

A) Doubt in the things of Lord God
B) Confusion in the things of Lord God
C) Mistrust in the things of Lord God
D) All of the above

Genesis 3:1–6

Note

In Genesis 3:4–5 Satan blinded Eve's mind with doubt:
"Has God said?"
"Ye shall surely not die ..."
"God knows in the day ye eat ..."
Read 2 Corinthians 4:3–4. Eve became a nonbeliever in God because she listened to the voice of Satan. Eve's doubt caused her not to be able to discern truth. In Genesis 3:6 she allowed her lustful desire to be wise to move her out of the will of God for her life. Read James 1:14–15. Satan, knowing what lust and disobedience would do, misled Eve.

29. Where was the man when his wife was being misled by the Serpent?

A) Sleeping
B) Tilling the garden
C) Talking with God
D) Standing with his wife and the Serpent

Genesis 3:2–6

30. After the woman ate from the forbidden tree and nothing happened, she gave some to her husband, who also ate. What happened after the man ate from the tree?

A) Nothing happened
B) Both of them died instantly
C) Their eyes were opened to their nakedness
D) Both B and C

Genesis 3:6–7

Think

Q. What did man get by eating from the Tree of the Knowledge of Good and Evil?
A. The knowledge of how to disobey, go against, Lord God. Romans 6:16–18 says, "Ye are a servant to whom ye obey." Luke 20:34–38 says, "God is the God of the living." Matthew 8:22 says, "Let the dead bury the dead." RTB. Man was created as a living soul. His disobedience to Lord God caused man to become a dying soul.

Think

Q. Why didn't anything happen when the woman ate the fruit?

A. The command was to man, not woman. According to Genesis 2:15, Adam's duty was to guard and keep the garden. Adam had authority to rebuke Eve and the Serpent. Note in Genesis 3 the Serpent was speaking to what would not happen to the woman.

Genesis 2:16–17

31. Who did the woman blame for her eating of the forbidden fruit?

A) Herself
B) Adam
C) The Serpent
D) Man

Genesis 3:13

Note

It wasn't until man disobeyed his authority figure that death opened their eyes to good and evil, according to Genesis 2:16–17. Death, good and evil, is the separation of God and man. Luke 20:38 says, "God is the God of the living, not the dead."

Note

Throughout the Bible it talks about people's eyes being opened and them having the ability to see things they first could not. For example, consider Hagar in Genesis 21:19 and Elisha in 2 Kings 6:17.

Note

Satan, the Evil One, opened the eyes of woman and man to the world of disobedience and sin, filling their minds and hearts with lust. The lust of the woman was for wisdom, and the lust of Adam was for the woman, which was a gift from Lord God.

They already had everything, but Satan blinded them with unbelief in what God said, the truth of God.

32. When asked by Lord God if Adam had eaten from the Tree of Knowledge of Good and Evil, who did man blame for eating of the forbidden fruit?

A) The woman
B) God
C) The Serpent
D) Both A and B

Genesis 3:11–12

33. What did Lord God do to the Serpent that had tricked and deceived the woman?

A) Nothing
B) Killed it
C) Cursed it
D) Sent it away

Genesis 3:14

34. Because man did not honor the authority figure in his life, Lord God, what did Lord God do?

A) He guarded all the trees he didn't want eaten.
B) He cursed the ground.
C) He made man work.
D) All of the above

Genesis 3:17

35. Lord God rebuked man for disobeying His command to not eat of the Tree of Knowledge of Good and Evil in the garden of Eden. What did He do to man?

A) He said he would struggle to farm the soil.
B) He said he would one day die.
C) He sent him out of the garden of Eden.
D) All of the above

Genesis 3:17–24

36. What was the punishment for man if he ate from the Tree of the Knowledge of Good and Evil according to Genesis 2:17?

A) Power
B) Grace
C) Death
D) Glory

Genesis 2:17

Think

Q. Why would the punishment be death for man's sins if according to John 8:1–11 the Lord does not condemn for sin?

A. He never planned for man to die.

Note

In Genesis 2:17 Lord God was explaining to man that he would surely die, be without God.

Sin
The wages of sin are death (Romans 6:23).

RTB

37. After eating of the Tree of Knowledge of Good and Evil, what other tree did Lord God not want man to eat of?

A) The Tree of Life
B) The Tree of Wisdom
C) The Tree of Death
D) All of the above

Genesis 3:22–24

Think

Q. Why didn't Lord God want man to eat from the Tree of Life after he sinned?

A. Humankind would have had to remain in a state of death for eternity.

Note

God had a plan for redemption. "For God so loved the world that He gave His only begotten Son" (John 3:16). He had plans to redeem and restore all creation that desired to fellowship with Him and not evil. The fall of Satan corrupted all of earth, according to Genesis 6:11–12. Lord God, knowing all things, knew what Satan would do to the physical man in the garden of Eden. Jeremiah 29:11 says God knows the plan and purpose for your life. Adam's was so that the Son of God could be born in fl and blood and redeem all (Genesis 3:15). Although many have been taught the exile of Adam from the garden was grace and mercy or just a separation from God, but Lord God continued to communicate with man.

38. Adam named his wife Eve. What does Eve mean in the Bible?

A) Beautiful woman
B) The mother of all living
C) Evening time
D) Both B and C

Genesis 3:20

39. Who was driven out of the garden in Genesis 3:24?

A) Adam
B) Adam and Eve
C) Man
D) All of the above

Genesis 3:24

Think

Q. Why does it say He drove out the man and not Adam?

A. He told man (living soul) not to eat of the tree. Man did not have a name at that time (Genesis 2:16–17).

The living soul wasn't named Adam until Genesis 2:19.

Note

Consider society's phrase "the *real* you," who lives on the inside, the living soul. The outer or physical you is what you physically see when you look at a person and associate his or her birth name, like Adam, with that individual. The soul (mind, will, and emotions) is what lives forever (Ecclesiastes 12:7). Lord God was talking to the living soul. This gives us more insight as to why we have memories of being on earth when we leave and why the decisions we make here matter. The real you, the living soul, lives forever, and it makes the decisions. (Read Luke 16:19–31.)

Note

Notice in Genesis 3:5 the serpent said that man and woman would become as gods, knowing good and evil by eating from the tree. This was a spiritual transformation. Lord God confirmed this was so in Genesis 3:22.

RTB
Lord God did not want man to stay evil.

40. After the man was driven out of the garden, what was placed at the entrance to protect the Tree of Life?

A) Angels and a sword
B) Creatures
C) Cherubims and a sword
D) Both A and C

Genesis 3:24

41. What were the names of Adam and Eve's first two sons?

A) Enoch and Seth
B) Cain and Abel
C) Noah and Joseph
D) None of the above

Genesis 4:1–2

42. Eve's firstborn son by Adam was named the following:

A) Seth
B) Cain
C) Abel
D) None of the above

Genesis 4:1

43. The first man ever born on earth was the following:

A) Adam
B) Abel
C) Cain
D) Seth

Genesis 4:1

44. Cain (the firstborn son of Adam and Eve) became the following:

A) A shepherd
B) A farmer
C) A musician
D) None of the above

Genesis 4:2

45. Abel (the second-born son of Adam and Eve) became the following:

A) A shepherd
B) A farmer
C) A musician
D) None of the above

Genesis 4:2

Note

Notice the profession Cain chose— to till the ground— ironically the very one Lord God created for man to do.

Genesis 4:2

46. Cain and Abel brought offerings to Lord God. Cain brought of the fruit of the ground, and Abel brought the firstlings of his flock and of the fat. Whose offerings did Lord God accept?

A) Abel's
B) Cain's
C) Abel's and Cain's
D) None of the above

Genesis 4:3–5

Think

Q. What was wrong with Cain's offering?

A. It was an insult because it came from the ground, which God had cursed. Often people believe their works and worthiness earn them righteousness and favor with God. However, the Bible reveals differently.

47. What did Cain do when Lord God refused his offering?

A) Became angry and indignant
B) Became wroth, and his countenance fell
C) Became sad and depressed
D) All of the above

Genesis 4:4–5

Think

Q. Why did Cain get upset and give Lord God attitude?

A. He fully understood what Lord God would accept as an offering, and he chose not to obey.

Note

Cain wanted to do things through self-worth, the work of his own hand, and still have fellowship with Lord God. Lord God shows the only way to Him is through obedience to the things He says.

Genesis 4:6–7

48. What did Lord God say would happen if Cain chose to obey?

A) He would reject him.
B) He would accept him.
C) He would have to repent.
D) None of the above

Genesis 4:7

49. What did Lord God say would happen if Cain did not obey?

A) He would reject him.
B) He would accept him.
C) Sin would lie at the door.
D) He would spew him out of His presence.

Genesis 4:6-7

Lord God states that sin desires Cain. However, Cain must rule over it and deny it what it wants. Notice how Lord God was warning Cain that his thoughts would cause him to sin.

50. Cain became very angry with his brother, Abel, because of the following reason:

A) Abel was Eve's favorite son.
B) Adam spent more time with Abel.
C) Abel's gift to the Lord was accepted, and Cain's gift to the Lord was rejected.
D) All of the above

Genesis 4:3–5

51. Cain got jealous and angry because the Lord rejected his gift but accepted Abel's gift. What sin did Cain commit as a result of his feelings?

A) He stopped speaking to his brother.
B) He beat his brother up.
C) He killed his brother, Abel.
D) Both A and B

Genesis 4:8

52. When the Lord asked Cain where his brother, Abel, was, Cain said the following:

A) "He's out in the field."
B) "He's home with Mom."
C) "I killed him."
D) "I know not."

Genesis 4:9

Note

Lord God was giving Cain an opportunity to repent just as He did with man after man ate from the Tree of the Knowledge of Good and Evil.

Think

Q. Why does Lord God ask questions of people when He knows all things?

A. It is an opportunity for individual reflection and repentance.

Many times an individual will do something he or she had an instinct not to do and regretted it later. God warned Cain in Genesis 4:6–7 to consider his thoughts and ways and in which direction they were taking him.

53. What brought the curse on Cain?

A) Attitude
B) Murder
C) Sin
D) Hatred

Genesis 4:5–8

54. The Lord punished Cain for killing his brother, Abel, and for lying about doing it. What was his punishment?

A) He was driven away from the land he killed his brother on.
B) No longer would the ground produce any food for him.
C) He would be a fugitive and a vagabond everywhere he went.
D) All of the above

Genesis 4:10–16

Note

Notice that Cain added words to what Lord God said in Genesis 4:14, "That everyone that findeth me shall slay me." A person can have what he or she says or asks for according to the will of God (Jeremiah 29:11– 14).

However, that wasn't God's will for Cain. So God set a course of

vengeance and placed a mark upon Cain to preserve his life.

55. What did Cain say after receiving his punishment for sin?

A) "I should have repented."
B) "Father, forgive me."
C) "My punishment is greater than I can bear."
D) "I should have listened and obeyed."

Genesis 4:13

56. When Cain later found a wife and had children, his wife came from the following:

A) God, who had created other people
B) Adam and Eve, who had daughters
C) None of the above
D) God formed a woman from his rib

Genesis 4:17 and 5:1–4

57. How many wives did Lamech have?

A) One
B) Two
C) None
D) One wife and one mistress

Genesis 4:19

Note

Notice the term *knew* in reference to a sexual union between husband and wife. However, there are several times the term *unto* was used where sexual relations took place that were not viewed as unions by God.

58. Adam and Eve had a third son named Seth, who they believed replaced the following:

A) Cain
B) Abel
C) Enos
D) None of the above

Genesis 4:25–26

59. Jabal, a descendant of Cain, became the first of the following:

A) Musician and inventor of the harp and organ
B) Cattleman and the first to live in tents
C) Instructor of every artificer (skilled workman) in brass and iron
D) None of the above

Genesis 4:20

60. Jubal (brother to Jabal), a descendant of Cain, became the first of the following:

A) Musician and inventor of the harp and organ
B) Cattleman and the first to live in tents
C) Instructor of every artificer (skilled workman) in brass and iron
D) All of the above

Genesis 4:21

61. Tubal-cain, a descendant of Cain, became the first of the following:

A) Musician and inventor of the harp and organ
B) Cattleman and the first to live in tents
C) Instructor of every artificer (skilled workman) in brass and iron
D) Both A and B

Genesis 4:22

62. To whom do men call upon?

A) Satan
B) God
C) Lord
D) Jesus

Genesis 4:26

Note

Consider Matthew 7:22–23. Why would the Lord say this? And notice He did not call Himself *Jesus* but *Lord*.

Think

Genesis 1:26–27

God said He would make a *man* in His *image* and *likeness*. This *man* was created male and female.

God Himself takes on male and female roles in the Bible. The *them* were given dominion over the earth and were told to multiply.

Think

Lesbian, Gay, Bisexual, and Transgender people are those whom the world classifies as such.

How can an LGBT male or female naturally multiply as God commands within others that are LGBT and stay in obedience to God? Review the apostle Paul's address in Romans 1:18-28 and God's in Genesis 19.

63. Which *man* is being spoken of in Genesis 5:1?

A) The *man* from Genesis 1
B) The *man* from Genesis 2
C) Both the Genesis 1 and Genesis 2 man
D) A spiritual man

Genesis 1:26 and 2:7

64. What is the name of the *man* in Genesis 1?

A) Man
B) Adam
C) Both A and B
D) None of the above

Genesis 5:2

65. What is the name of the man created in Genesis 2?

A) Man
B) Adam
C) Both A and B
D) None of the above

Genesis 2:19

Note

This may bring insight to those who have been taught that there was a first and second Adam.

66. Adam's son Seth produced children, and they produced children through the years until Lamech was born. Lamech was 182 years old when the following occurred:

A) Enoch was born
B) Jared was born
C) Noah was born
D) None of the above

Genesis 5:28–29

67. How old was Noah when he had Shem, Ham, and Japheth?

A) Three hundred years old
B) Four hundred years old
C) Five hundred years old
D) Between B and C

Genesis 5:32

Note

When God formed man, He made man perfect. The body was created to live forever. Sin is what brought death. In later text you will see where God shortens man's life span.

68.. At five hundred years old Noah had three sons. What were their names?

A) Shem, Ham, and Japheth
B) Jabal, Jubal, and Tubal-cain
C) Cain, Abel, and Seth
D) Shem, Jabal, and Cain

Genesis 5:32

69. Whom did the sons of God see?

A) Angels
B) Eve
C) Daughters of men
D) Sons of men

Genesis 6:2

Note

There are two classes of beings in Genesis 6:2. The sons of God saw the daughters of men, and they took them as wives. This was not a union God joined together. "They took them wives of all which they chose." In Genesis 6:4 notice these were sons of God and not sons of men. They too have DNA and reproducing power! Children are images of their parents.

R T B

Note

Remember God's command in Genesis 1 was for them to mate with each other and multiply in the earth. Then in Genesis 2 the man formed from the ground didn't have a suitable mate Genesis 2:18 until God formed the woman from his rib and took her out of man (Genesis 2:22-23).

70. Why was Lord God's Holy Spirit striving with the man?

A) Because of man's disobedience
B) Because of evil spirits
C) Because of man's flesh
D) All of the above

Genesis 6:3

Think

Q. Why would the Lord God in Genesis 6:3 say the man He is striving with is *also* flesh? The Bible already reflects that the Genesis 2 man has flesh.

A. The *man* formed in Genesis 1:27 had some form of flesh. (Notice if your Bible has a concordance, it references Genesis 1:28.)

R T B

Note

There are religious organizations that teach that the flesh is a mind- set that goes against God, appealing to their own impulses and the desires of their carnal nature. A carnal mind is the thought process of the brain and the imagination. The brain is the enemy of God (Romans 8:7–10). Further examination of the thought process should be read in 1 Peter 3:21.

Think

It may be difficult to read that the enemy of God is one with a carnal mind. That is why man's life span was shortened—so much so that it required the flood of the entire earth, ending life for all except those in the ark.

Keep reading the Bible.

71. God didn't want to strive with man forever. So what did He do to the man?

A) Killed him
B) Cursed him
C) Shortened his life span
D) None of the above

Genesis 6:3

72. How many years did God say man should live?

A) 120
B) 90
C) 60
D) Eternity

Genesis 6:3

73. Which *man* got his life shortened?

A) Genesis 1 man
B) Genesis 2 man
C) Both A and B
D) None, because of grace

Genesis 6:3 and 25:7

74. The offspring of sons of God and daughters of men were what?

A) Blessed
B) Evil
C) Men of renown
D) Men of God

Genesis 6:4

75. Who saw the wickedness of man as great in the earth and that every imagination of the thought of his heart was only evil continually?

A) Lord God
B) God
C) Man
D) Holy Spirit

Genesis 6:5

76. Who repented and was grieved at the heart for making man on the earth?

A) Holy Spirit
B) God
C) Lord God
D) All of the above

Genesis 6:6

77. The Lord said He was going to destroy man, beasts, and animals. Why?

A) Because the sons of God and man had made a mess
B) Because of the corruption of thought and wickedness in man's heart
C) Because God wanted to regain control of the earth
D) All of the above

Genesis 6:5

78. Which man did the Lord repent and grieve that he made?

A) The one in Genesis 1:26 in His image and likeness
B) The one in Genesis 2:7 formed from the dust of the ground
C) Both A and B
D) None of the above

Genesis 6:6–7

79. In the days of Noah, God planned to destroy mankind except for Noah. Why?

A) He was a descendant of Adam.
B) He was an old wise man.
C) Noah found grace in the eyes of the Lord.
D) Both B and C

Genesis 6:7–9

80. How did Noah find grace with Lord God?

A) He was a just man.
B) He was perfect in his generation.
C) He walked with God.
D) All of the above

Genesis 6:9

81. What was wrong with the earth in the sight of God in Genesis 6?

A) It was void and empty.
B) It was full of hate and greed.
C) It was corrupt and filled with violence.
D) It was full of selfishness and not love.

Genesis 6:11

82. In the book of Genesis, what had corrupted itself upon the earth?

A) Man
B) Animals
C) All flesh
D) The Spirit

Genesis 6:12

83. Why did God choose to destroy all those who were among the earth?

A) Because of corruption
B) Because of violence
C) Because of lust
D) Because of disobedience

Genesis 6:13

Think

Consider what type of violence could have been going on at that time.

Then consider the violence of today. Next consider God's solution or justice for the problem.

Matthew 24:33–44, 2 Peter 3:3–10

84. What did God command Noah to do to save him and his family from the floodwaters?

A) Climb the east mountain
B) Stay indoors
C) Build an ark
D) Tell everyone

Genesis 6:14–16

85. In the days of Noah, how was God planning to destroy all mankind on earth?

A) With fire and brimstone from heaven
B) With a flood of waters
C) With mighty earthquakes
D) With destruction of all flesh

Genesis 6:17

86. Who did God say He would establish His covenant with in Genesis 6?

A) Adam
B) Noah
C) *Them*
D) All of the above

Genesis 6:13–18

87. What and/or who did God say to bring on the ark besides Noah's family?

A) Two of every kind of animal and bug
B) Two of every living thing of all flesh
C) Genesis 1 man and Genesis 2 man
D) All of the above

Genesis 6:19

88. Why did God tell Noah to allow every living thing of all flesh to come on the ark with him?

A) For food
B) To keep them alive
C) To let them to multiply on the earth again
D) All of the above

Genesis 6:19

Note

Noah lost or left everything he had except his family. God didn't tell him to bring any personal belongs with him.

Genesis 6:22

89. Why did God honor Noah and his family with preservation of life? Because Noah was _____ before God:

A) Obedient
B) Walking in love
C) Honorable
D) Righteous

Genesis 7:1

90. How many clean and unclean pairs of beasts was Noah told to bring on the ark, the male and his female?

A) By seven and two
B) By two and two
C) By Two and seven
D) Noah and his family only

Genesis 7:2

Note

Noah did all that God commanded him to do, and all who were with him were saved.

91. Noah was how old when the floodwaters came?

A) 550 years old
B) 600 years old
C) 650 years old
D) Between A and B

Genesis 7:6

92. After Noah, his family, and two of every sort of living thing of all flesh were on the ark, how many days was it before God closed the door?

A) 3 days
B) 7 days
C) 14 days
D) 150 days

Genesis 7:10

93. How long did the Lord cause it to rain while Noah was on the ark?

A) 150 days and 150 nights
B) 40 days and 40 nights
C) 26 days and 25 nights
D) None of the above

Genesis 7:11–12

94. Did the Genesis 1 man get on the ark that Noah built?

A) Yes
B) No

Genesis 7:15–16

95. How high did the water bring the ark?

A) Above the earth
B) As high as the tallest mountain
C) Fifteen cubits upward
D) It stayed dry where the ark was.

Genesis 7:17

96. According to the Bible, what was used to destroy everything on earth in the book of Genesis?

A) Fire
B) Diseases
C) Weapons
D) Water

Genesis 7:19–21

Note

There is a lot of speculation as to how high or deep the water was. Genesis 6:17 states everything in the earth would die by flood.

RTB

Note

Here are a few things to ponder. Genesis 5:20 says that the water was fifteen cubits upward and the mountains were covered. First, birds flew in the air, and they died according to Genesis 7:21. Second, the ark was on top of the water, which bore it up so high it was above the earth (outer space) according to Genesis 7:17.

RTB

97. During the Genesis 6 flood, did the fish die?

A) Yes
B) No

Genesis 7:21–23

98. How long did the waters prevail upon the earth?

A) 40 days
B) 150 days
C) 26 days
D) None of the above

Genesis 7:24

99. After all in the land were destroyed in the flood of Genesis, how did God move the water?

A) He spoke to it.
B) He used his hands.
C) He used wind.
D) All of the above

Genesis 8:1

100. What area of land did the ark finally rest on?

A) The mountains of Ararat
B) The mountains of Africa
C) The mountains of Asia
D) The mountains of Afghanistan

Genesis 8:4

101. During the Genesis flood, in what month did the top of the mountains begin to be seen?

    A) First month
    B) Eighth month
    C) Ninth month
    D) Tenth month

Genesis 8:5

Think

Genesis 8:6 says, "At the end of forty days that Noah opened the window of the ark." This is not the forty days and forty nights from the time the ark rested on the mountains of Ararat, which some say is modern-day Turkey.

R T B

102. How many animals did Noah send out of the ark to check to see if the ground was dry?

    A) One
    B) Two
    C) Four
    D) Eight

Genesis 8:7–8

103. How long was Noah on the ark before he opened the door of the ark?

    A) Forty days and forty nights
    B) One year
    C) Eighty days
    D) One year and fifty-seven days

Genesis 7:6 and 8:13

104. How long did Noah and everybody with him stay in the ark after Noah removed the covering before God spoke and told him to come out?

They came out at the following time:

    A) Immediately
    B) After forty days
    C) After ten months
    D) After one month and twenty-seven days

Genesis 8:13–17

105. What was the first thing Noah did when he got off the ark?

    A) Partied
    B) Took a bath
    C) Ran praising God
    D) Built an altar

Genesis 8:18–20

106. What did the Lord say in His *heart* concerning man's *heart*?

A) It is envious and jealous.
B) It is evil from his youth.
C) It is easily distorted.
D) All of the above

Genesis 8:21

107. When God stopped the rain and the land became dry, Noah, his family, and all the animals in the ark came out. What was God's promise for the earth?

A) To never again curse the ground because of man
B) To never again kill every living thing
C) While the earth remained, seed-time and harvest, cold and heat, summer and winter, and day and night shall not cease.
D) All of the above

Genesis 8:20–22

108. After Noah came out of the ark, God told him and his family to do the following:

A) Build a great city
B) Eat only vegetables and seafood
C) Replenish the earth
D) All of the above

Genesis 9:1

Note

Notice how the things that God did not authorize authority over—such as seed-time and harvest, summer and winter, day and night—He said would never cease while the earth remains.

Note

During these times it was not unlawful to marry, union with, family members. It became unlawful in Leviticus 18:6.

Note

In the beginning, dominion was given to the Genesis 1 man according to Genesis 1:28.

109. In Genesis 9 God was establishing order. Who was given control, authority, or dominion over all the earth?

A) Genesis 1 man
B) Genesis 2 man
C) Noah and his sons
D) All of the above

Genesis 9:1–2

110. What were Noah and his sons forbidden to eat?

A) Animals
B) People
C) Blood
D) Both B and C

Genesis 9:4–5

111. What is the punishment for taking a man's life according to Genesis 9:5–6?

A) Death
B) Forgiveness
C) Revenge
D) Damnation

Ponder on whom is the *"you"* in Genesis 9:7, for God spoke unto Noah and his sons in Genesis 9:8. So who is He speaking to in Genesis 9:7—the animals, plants, birds, and/ or Genesis 1 man?

112. According to Genesis 9:11, God established His covenant with Noah that all flesh would never be cut off anymore by what?

A) Fire
B) Disease
C) Flood
D) Wind

Genesis 9:11

The Bible doesn't say that all flesh would never be cut off again from the earth. Also notice there were no commandments given to prevent the darkness that caused the flood in the first place.

God created us with the ability to choose good or bad, right or wrong.

Deuteronomy 30:19

113. What was placed within the clouds as a token sign that when clouds come over the earth, that they wouldn't flood the earth?

A) An array of colors
B) A bow
C) Jesus
D) The sun

Genesis 9:12–17

114. Who were the three sons of Noah who repopulated the entire earth?

A) Shem, Ham, and Japheth
B) Abraham, Isaac, and Jacob
C) Shadrach, Meshach, and Abednego
D) Cain, Abel, and Seth

Genesis 9:17–19

115. God asked Noah to gather every kind of creature on the ark for the following reason:

A) So they wouldn't be alone.
B) So they could reproduce.
C) So they would live.
D) None of the above

Genesis 6:17–20

116. Noah cursed his grandson Canaan because his son Ham did what?

A) Ham was disobedient.
B) Ham lied to his father.
C) Ham saw his father's nakedness.
D) All of the above

Genesis 9:20–25

117. How old was Noah when he died?

A) 99
B) 950
C) 350
D) 40

Genesis 9:28–29

118. Noah's sons' children repopulated the earth after the great flood. The people did the following:

A) Developed their own language
B) Spoke one language
C) Both A and B
D) None of the above

Genesis 11:1

119. Why were the people building a tower to reach heaven?

A) To make a name for themselves
B) So that they wouldn't be scattered over the whole earth
C) To please God
D) Both A and B

Genesis 11:4

120. In Genesis 11 what did the Lord do to prevent the people from building a tower they thought could reach heaven?

A) He confounded (mixed up) their language.
B) He told them to stop.
C) He caused the tower to fall.
D) All of the above

Genesis 11:4–8

121. Did the Lord have help confounding the people's language?

A) Yes
B) No

Genesis 11:7

122. Who built the city that caused the Lord to create multiple languages?

A) Noah and his sons
B) Children of God
C) Children of men
D) Both B and C

Genesis 11:5

123. What was the name of the city where the Lord confused the languages of earth?

A) Tyre
B) Bethlehem
C) Babel
D) Sidon

Genesis 11:9

124. What was the name of Abram's father?

A) Palag
B) Reu
C) Nahor
D) Terah

Genesis 11:27

125. Haran, Abram's brother, had a son named the following:

A) Nahor
B) Lot
C) Terah
D) None of the above

Genesis 11:27

126. In Genesis 11 Abram's wife was named:

A) Milcah
B) Sarai
C) Hara
D) None of the above

Genesis 11:29

127. In the beginning of marriage, what was wrong with Sarai, Abram's wife?

A) She lacked faith.
B) She was unattractive.
C) She was a burden.
D) She was barren.

Genesis 11:30

128. Who took Abram and Sarai to the land of Canaan?

A) Abram
B) Terah
C) Haran
D) Lot

Genesis 11:31

129. Abram took his wife, Sarai, and his possessions and left his land. Why?

A) There were too many people there.
B) The Lord told him to.
C) He did not like his neighbors.
D) All of the above

Genesis 12:1

130. When Abram left his land with his family and possessions, what did God promise him?

A) He would bless him greatly.
B) A great nation out of Abram would form.
C) The name of Abram would be great.
D) All of the above

Genesis 12:1–3

131. Because of Abram, whose family would be blessed?

A) Abram's family
B) Lot's family
C) Terah's family
D) All families of the earth

Genesis 12:3

Note

Abram was obeying God and leaving, and Lot chose to go with him.

132. How old was Abram when he left his country and relatives?

A) 99
B) 75
C) 120
D) 38

Genesis 12:4

133. Why did Abram go to Egypt?

A) To overtake it
B) To live there
C) To avoid famine
D) Both B and C

Genesis 12:10

134. Entering Egypt, what did Abram tell his wife because of her beauty?

A) Pretend to be my daughter.
B) Pretend to be my sister.
C) Do not look directly at the men.
D) None of the above

Genesis 12:10–13

135. What was Abram afraid of when he and Sarai approached Egypt?

A) The Egyptians would want his wife.
B) He would be killed for Sarai.
C) None of the above
D) Both A and B

Genesis 12:11–13

136. The pharaoh of Egypt considered Abram's wife to be his wife. What did God do because of this?

A) Told Pharaoh to give her back
B) Plagued Pharaoh and his house
C) Blessed him with children
D) Both A and B

Genesis 12:14–17

Note

It is important to note that during these times, those who were married as husbands and wives were also relatives of each other. Sarai was also Abram's half-sister (Genesis 20:12).

R T B

137. Abram was the following:

A) Poor
B) Rich
C) Enemies with Lot
D) Both A and C

Genesis 13:2–6

138. Why did Abram separate himself and his possessions from his nephew, Lot, and Lot's possessions?

A) Their combined possessions were too great.
B) Their herdsmen were fighting.
C) The land could not bear them.
D) All of the above

Genesis 13:6–9

139. Why didn't Abram want strife between him and Lot?

A) Lot was like a son.
B) They both had great possessions.
C) They were brethren (relatives).
D) All of the above

Genesis 13:8

Note

When it was time to separate, Lot became selfish and chose the land that visibly looked better (Genesis 13:10).

140. What area of land did Lot choose?

A) The land of Canaan
B) The plains of Jordan
C) Sodom and Gomorrah
D) The plain of Mamre

Genesis 13:11

Note

The plain of Jordan was near Sodom and Gomorrah, and the men dwelling there were exceedingly wicked.

Genesis 13:12–13

141. What land did the Lord promise to give Abram and his seed (children)?

A) The land of Canaan
B) The land of Sodom
C) The land of Gomorrah
D) All land

Genesis 13:12–15

Note

Notice how God waited until Lot had separated from Abram to remind Abram of His promise of possessing all the land.

142. When Abram learned that his nephew, Lot, was taken captive from Sodom and the other kings in battle had fled, what did Abram do?

A) He prayed for Lot's safe return.
B) He armed his men and pursued Lot's captors.
C) He did nothing.
D) None of the above

Genesis 14:12–16

Note

After Abram's victory, the king of Sodom and the other kings as well as Melchizedek, king of Salem, came to meet Abram and reward him for their victory.

Genesis 14:17–19

143. What did Melchizedek give Abram for winning his battle?

A) All that he brought back
B) All the people he saved
C) Tithes of all
D) Nothing

Genesis 14:20

144. What did the king of Sodom offer Abram for winning his battle?

A) All the people he saved
B) All the goods he brought back
C) Tithes of all
D) Nothing

Genesis 14:21–24

Note

Notice how the king of Sodom's offering was not accepted and the offering of Melchizedek, king of Salem, was. Ponder on the offerings of Cain and Abel.

Genesis 14:20–24 and 4:3–7

145. In Genesis 15 Abram was having a conversation with the Lord concerning him being childless and asking who would be his heir. Who was the steward of Abram's house?

A) Lot
B) Peleg
C) Eber
D) Eliezer

Genesis 15:2

146. Abram believed in the Lord's capability to provide him a child of his own. The Lord viewed his belief as what?

A) Faith
B) Hope
C) Righteousness
D) All of the above

Genesis 15:6

Note

Abram only believed, and it was viewed by Lord God as righteous. He did not earn it by any physical act.

147. The Lord gave Abram a prophecy of the future of his descendants. What was it?

A) They would be strangers in a land not their own.
B) They would be servants.
C) They would be afflicted for four hundred years.
D) All of the above

Genesis 15:12–14

148. Why did Sarai offer her maid (Hagar) to her husband, Abram, as a second wife?

A) She was young and beautiful.
B) She wanted to please her husband.
C) She wanted Abram to have children, which she couldn't give him.
D) All of the above

Genesis 16:1–2

Note

Abram hearkened to the voice of Sarai and went in and conceived a child with the handmaid.

Genesis 16:4–6

149. Why did Sarai deal harshly with Hagar after Hagar got pregnant?

A) Because Sarai was jealous
B) Because Abram did not want the child
C) Because Hagar despised Sarai
D) All of the above

Genesis 16:5

Note

Neither Abram nor the Bible ever acknowledged Hagar as Abram's second wife. The Bible only states he went in (had intercourse) with Hagar.

The study of Genesis 25 reveals he later had another wife after the death of Sarai.

150. Why did Hagar, who was pregnant with Abram's child, flee from his wife, Sarai?

A) Hagar feared for her life.
B) Sarai dealt harshly with her.
C) Abram told her to.
D) All of the above

Genesis 16:6

151. Who told Hagar to return to Sarai and submit herself?

A) Abram
B) Sarai
C) A priest
D) The angel of the Lord

Genesis 16:7–9

152. What did the angel of the Lord promise Hagar out in the wilderness?

A) She would have no more children.
B) She would lose the child she was having.
C) Her seed would be multiplied exceedingly.
D) None of the above

Genesis 16:7–10

Note

For obeying the voice of God, Hagar's seed/child would multiply exceedingly.

Think

Q. Who is the angel of the Lord?

A. The angel is Lord God, the only one capable of multiplying her seed. (There are several Bibles with notes reflecting the fact that Lord God appeared on earth in the form of the angel of the Lord during the Old Testament before Jesus Christ. This was the form of communication. They visually saw, touched, and could feel the Lord.)

153. How old was Abram when Hagar had his son?

A) Fourscore and six years old (eighty-six)
B) Fourscore and five years old (eighty-five)
C) Fourscore and four years old (eighty-four)
D) None of the above

Genesis 16:15–16

154. What name did the angel of the Lord tell Hagar to name her child, the son of Abram?

A) Jacob
B) Ishmael
C) Isaac
D) None of the above

Genesis 16:11–15

155. In Genesis 17 the Lord appeared unto Abram. What did He tell him he had to do to be perfect?

A) Walk before the Lord
B) Tithe
C) Sin not
D) All of the above

Genesis 17:1

156. Abram's covenant to walk before the Lord made him what?

A) Righteous
B) Blameless
C) Smart
D) A father of many nations

Genesis 17:4

157. When Abram was ninety-nine years old, the Lord changed his name to the following:

A) Isaac
B) Abraham
C) Jacob
D) Peter

Genesis 17:5

158. As a part of Abraham's covenant with God, what else was required?

A) He could never sin.
B) Every man-child should be circumcised.
C) The adoption of strangers for money
D) The sacrifice of every man child

Genesis 17:9–11

159. When is the earliest time at which a male should be circumcised according to the covenant with Abraham?

A) At birth
B) At eight days old
C) Never
D) At three days old

Genesis 17:12

160. What is said of the man/ soul who chose not to be circumcised?

A) He shall be cut off from his people
B) He has broken God's covenant.
C) He shall die.
D) Both A and B

Genesis 17:14

161. Abram's name was changed to Abraham by God. What was his wife Sarai's name changed to?

A) Serena
B) Sarah
C) Deborah
D) None of the above

Genesis 17:15–16

162. After God changed Sarai's name, what did He say he would give Sarah and Abraham?

A) The whole earth
B) Many nations
C) A blessing
D) A son

Genesis 17:16

163. Who did God say Sarah should be?

A) A mother of nations
B) A mother of the living
C) A mother of nature
D) A mother of tribes

Genesis 17:16

164. Read Genesis 17:16–17. From this passage, it's easy to conclude the following:

A) Abraham and Sarah really loved each other.
B) Sarah wanted to leave Abraham.
C) Abraham doubted he and Sarah could have a child at their age.
D) Both A and C

165. What did God say Abraham and Sarah's son's name should be?

A) Cain
B) Isaac
C) Ishmael
D) Lot

Genesis 17:19

166. Which son of Abraham received the everlasting covenant from God?

A) John
B) Ishmael
C) Jokshan
D) Isaac

Genesis 17:19

167. Which one of Abraham's sons produced twelve princes?

A) Isaac
B) Midian
C) Jokshan
D) Ishmael

Genesis 17:20

168. The Lord appeared to Abraham in the plains of Mamre. How many men were with him?

A) One
B) Two
C) Three
D) None. They were all the Lord.

Genesis 18:1–3

Note

After the men had eaten, washed their feet, and rested, the Bible says they asked, "Where is Sarah thy wife?" Remember God knows all; He knew she was at the tent door listening. This was an opportunity to clear doubt from their hearts concerning the promise of a son.

Genesis 18:4–9

169. How did Sarah laugh when the Lord told Abraham that Sarah would have a child?

A) In the Lord's face
B) Out loud in the tent
C) Under her breath
D) Within herself

Genesis 18:10–12

170. Sarah laughed at the Lord when He told Abraham they would have a child at their old age. What did the Lord say to that?

A) "Maybe I can't do it."
B) "Don't laugh at me."
C) "Is anything too hard for the Lord?"
D) "Why do you doubt my abilities?"

Genesis 18:13–14

Note

Our thoughts are known to God. Notice how the Lord was at the tent talking with Abraham in the form of a man who was capable of eating and drinking and heard what Sarah said within herself. (She uttered nothing.)

Certain Bibles reference this in amplified Bible notes at the bottom of the page.

171. Why did Sarah lie about laughing concerning having a child at her old age?

A) She was afraid of the Lord.
B) She thought a white lie wouldn't hurt anybody.
C) She didn't like being questioned about her actions.
D) She just couldn't help herself.

Genesis 18:15

172. Why were the men and the Lord headed to Sodom and Gomorrah?

A) The cry was great.
B) The sin was very grievous.
C) The depression was severe.
D) Both A and B

Genesis 18:20

173. The Lord told Abraham the sins of Sodom and Gomorrah were great; Abraham talked the Lord into sparing the cities of them who were just the following:

A) Thirty righteous in the whole city
B) Twenty righteous in the whole city
C) Ten righteous in the whole city
D) All of the above

Genesis 18:22–32

174. Two men (who were angels) approached Lot at the city of Sodom. What did Lot do?

A) He turned them away.
B) He invited them to his home.
C) He gave them directions.
D) Both B and C

Genesis 18:22 and Genesis 19:1–3

Note

Notice how both Abraham and Lot identified the men approaching them (as Lord and angels) and treated them very similarly by providing a resting spot, food, and a place to wash their feet.

175. All the men of the city and all the men of Sodom wanted the men Lot brought into his home to come out. Why?

A) They wanted to talk to them.
B) They wanted to do wicked things to them (know them).
C) They wanted them to leave the city.
D) None of the above

Genesis 19:4–7

Note

There are several incidents where the term *know* or *knew* is referred to in a sexual manner where there was no marriage union refer to amplified bible. Notice in Genesis 19:8 Lot offers his two virgin daughters to the mob of men. The men respond hastily as though Lot is being their judge. Also remember that Lot dwelled in the plains of Jordan near Sodom and Gomorrah.

RTB

176. Lot tried to offer his daughters to the wicked men, but they did the following:

A) Refused them, for they wanted the men
B) Accepted them and did as they pleased
C) Kept only one daughter
D) None of the above

Genesis 19:8–9

177. What happened after the wicked men felt Lot was judging them for wanting to have intercourse with the men (angels) in his house?

A) They threatened him.
B) They raped him.
C) They died immediately.
D) They asked for forgiveness.

Genesis 19:9

RTB

32

Think

Why would the wicked men even think they could have intercourse with angels in the form of men? Refer back to Genesis 6:2.

R T B

178. After the wicked men threatened Lot, what did the men in the house do?

A) Put forth their hands
B) Shut the door
C) Smote them with blindness
D) All of the above

Genesis 19:10–11

179. What happened when Lot tried to convince his sons-in-law that Sodom was being destroyed?

A) They left with him.
B) They mocked him (didn't believe).
C) They convinced Lot to stay.
D) Both B and C

Genesis 19:14

Note

Notice the mercy of God in Genesis 19:15–17 despite Lot's slackness to do what he was told. He was moments away from death, but because of the prayers of Abraham, his life was spared despite his lack of urgency.

Note

Lot was still being difficult even after he identified his life had been spared through grace and mercy in Genesis 19:17–23. Notice the grace of God in man's ability to choose. God allowed Lot's desires to by permitting Lot to go to Zoar instead of the mountains.

180. What did God do to the wicked cities of Sodom and Gomorrah?

A) He rained brimstone and fire on the cities from heaven.
B) He ignored the cities.
C) He brought a great flood.
D) None of the above

Genesis 19:24–25

181. Lot, his wife, and his two daughters were warned not to look at the destruction of Sodom and Gomorrah. What happened to Lot's wife when she looked back?

A) She disappeared.
B) She turned into a pillar of salt.
C) She fell to the ground dead.
D) None of the above

Genesis 19:24–26

182. How many daughters did Lot take with him when he left Zoar?

A) One
B) Two
C) Three
D) Four

Genesis 19:30

183. Lot's wife died as a pillar of salt, cremated. Why did his daughters get him drunk?

A) They wanted to preserve the seed of Lot.
B) Their hearts were filled with lust.
C) They didn't want to be virgins any longer.
D) They wanted to see him drunk.

Genesis 19:32

184. Both of Lot's daughters bore him a son. Who are they the fathers of?

A) The Moabites and the Ammonites
B) The Canaanites and the Israelites
C) The Hivittes and the Amorites
D) The Temarites and the Hittites

Genesis 19:37–38

185. Why did Abimelech, king of Gerar, take Sarah the wife of Abraham?

A) Abimelech wanted Sarah for himself.
B) Abraham owed Abimelech for coming into Gerar.
C) Abraham said she was his sister.
D) Both A and C

Genesis 20:1–2

186. God told King Abimelech that Sarah was Abraham's wife through the following sign:

A) A vision
B) A dream
C) A burning bush
D) None of the above

Genesis 20:2–3

Note

Notice how God protected Abimelech from sinning against Him since Abimelech was being deceived by both Sarah and Abraham. Notice that despite Abraham and Sarah's doubt and unbelief that God would protect them as a couple, God continued to cover them and protect them and bring revealed truth to their deception. They thought they were outsmarting the people by saying they were brother and sister. However, God revealed the truth every time.

Genesis 20:10–12

187. God told King Abimelech that Abraham was the following:

A) A thief
B) A healer
C) A prophet
D) None of the above

Genesis 20:6–8

188. What did the Lord do to the house of Abimelech because Abimelech had taken Sarah, Abraham's wife, into his house?

A) Destroyed it
B) Caused plagues and famine on it
C) Fast closed all the wombs of the house
D) All of the above

Genesis 20:14–18

Note

Countless times the Bible shows God is in control of the womb of the woman.

Genesis 29:31
Genesis 30:2
Luke 1:7 and Luke 1:13–20
Luke1:27–31

189. The Lord gave Abraham a son by Sarah, as He had promised, in their old age. What was his name?

A) Jacob
B) Ishmael
C) Isaac
D) Matthew

Genesis 21:1–3

190. What was the name of the mother of Isaac?

A) Hagar
B) Sarah
C) Rebecca
D) None of the above

Genesis 21:1–3

191. Sarah saw Ishmael (Hagar's son) mocking Isaac. At Sarah's request, Abraham did the following:

A) Told Ishmael to stop
B) Sent Hagar and Ishmael away
C) Told Isaac to fight back
D) None of the above

Genesis 21:9–14

192. When did Abraham hearken to the voice and commands of Sarah?

A) Immediately
B) After he finished grieving
C) Never
D) After God said it was okay

Genesis 21:12

193. What two things did Abraham give the bondwoman before sending her and the lad away?

A) Bread and water
B) Food and light
C) Prayer and blessings
D) Bread and light

Genesis 21:14

194. When there was no water left, Hagar didn't want to see the child die. Where did she place the child?

A) In the wilderness
B) In the fire
C) Under one of the shrubs
D) Back with Abraham

Genesis 21:15

Note

In Genesis 21:17–20 notice God hears the voices of children as well as adults. Therefore, remember when all hope is lost and when quitting seems to be the only option, they too can lift up their voices to the heavens from which comes their help.

Note

Ishmael did nothing to earn greatness. It was God's will and desire and His plan and purpose for Ishmael's life. God said, "I will make him a great nation."

Genesis 21:18

195. When did Hagar see the well of water?

A) After the angel of God spoke to her
B) After she lifted up Ishmael
C) After God opened her eyes
D) All of the above

Genesis 21:19

196. Ishmael, son of Abraham, dwelt in the wilderness and became the following:

A) A carpenter
B) A blacksmith
C) An archer
D) None of the above

Genesis 21:20

197. God tempted Abraham's faith and obedience by telling Abraham to do the following:

A) Sacrifice his son Isaac
B) Kill his son Ishmael
C) Sacrifice his wife, Sarah
D) Both A and B

Genesis 22:1–2

God had already told Abraham Isaac's future. Abraham rested in knowing what God said in Genesis 22:5. His willingness to obey what God told him to do right then proved his reverent fear of God and faith in God.

Genesis 22:12

RTB

198. Because God had provided for not only Himself but for Abraham and Isaac, what did Abraham call that area of land?

A) Jehovah-Nissi
B) Jehovah-Jireh
C) Jehovah-Rapha
D) Jehovah

Genesis 22:13–14

God has several names that reflect his character, one of which is Jehovah-Jireh, which means "my provider" in Hebrew.

199. Because of the willingness of Abraham to sacrifice his only son (Isaac) to God as a burnt offering, God promised the following:

A) To bless Abraham abundantly
B) To multiply Abraham's seed as the stars in heaven
C) To punish Abraham for wanting to do such a thing
D) Both A and B

Genesis 22:15–18

200. How old was Sarah when she died?

A) 127
B) 120
C) 300
D) 99

Genesis 23:1

201. What is a sepulchre?

A) A cave
B) A tomb
C) A burial place
D) All of the above

Genesis 23:3–6

202. Sarah was buried in the cave of Machpelah. How much did Abraham pay for it?

A) Nothing
B) He paid nothing for the cave but four hundred shekels of silver for the land.
C) He paid four hundred shekels, which included the cave and the land.
D) Four hundred shekels for the cave but nothing for the land.

Genesis 23:9–20

Notice there was some form of money exchanged, not just goods exchanged for goods.

203. Abraham (getting old and stricken) made his eldest servant swear to find a wife for his son Isaac in the following location:

A) From among the Canaanites
B) From among the beautiful women of Egypt
C) From his own country and kindred
D) Any of the above

Genesis 24:1–4

204. Because the elder servant doubted in his ability to bring a wife back for Isaac, who did Abraham say would go in front of him and prepare the servant's way?

A) Isaac
B) An angel
C) Another servant
D) No one

Genesis 24:5–8

205. What did Abraham's elder servant, Eliezer, take with him on his journey?

A) A tenth of all Abraham's goods
B) Ten camels
C) Ten men
D) None of the above

Genesis 24:10

206. What did Abraham's elder servant pray for while on his way to find Isaac's wife?

A) A favor
B) A blessing
C) Help
D) Good speed (good success)

Genesis 24:12

Think

Did the Lord answer Abraham's prayer? Read Genesis 24:13–27.

207. Abraham was giving Isaac the following:

A) None of his possessions
B) Half of his possessions (Ishmael was getting the other half.)
C) All that he owned
D) None of the above

Genesis 24:34–36

208. What was the name of Abraham's niece, who was to become Isaac's wife?

A) Sarah
B) Deborah
C) Rebekah
D) None of the above

Genesis 24:48–51

209. How was Isaac comforted after the death of his mother, Sarah?

A) With a child
B) With his father's inheritance
C) By servants and handmaids
D) With a wife

Genesis 24:63–67

210. Abraham, a righteous man in God's eyes, died at 175 years old. Who buried him?

A) Isaac and Ishmael
B) Cain and Abel
C) Jacob and Nahor
D) All of the above

Genesis 25:7–9

211. The twins born to Isaac and Rebekah were named as follows:

A) Isaac and Ishmael
B) Esau and Jacob
C) Cain and Abel
D) None of the above

Genesis 25:23–26

212. Isaac's son Esau became a cunning hunter. Jacob became the following:

A) A hunter like Esau
B) A skilled blacksmith
C) A plain man dwelling in tents
D) A carpenter

Genesis 25:27

213. The younger brother, Jacob, tricked his older brother, Esau, into selling the following:

A) His bow and arrow
B) His herd of cattle
C) His chest of gold and silver
D) His birthright (inheritance)

Genesis 25:29–34

214. Why did God say he would bless Isaac in the land of Gerar?

A) Because he sowed into that land
B) Because of Abraham's obedience
C) Because of Isaac's obedience to God
D) Because of Isaac's faith

Genesis 26:1–5

Note

Notice how history repeats itself with Abraham and Isaac in Genesis 26.

215. At the age of forty, who did Esau take as his wife?

A) Judith
B) Bashemath
C) Judith and Bashemath
D) Deborah

Genesis 26:34

216. What does the Bible say about Esau and his choice to take a wife?

A) It was not an acceptable union.
B) It was a bitter struggle.
C) It was pleasing to all.
D) It brought grief of mind to his parents.

Genesis 26:34–35

217. Who did Isaac want to bless before he died?

A) Rebekah
B) Esau
C) Jacob
D) His family

Genesis 27:1–4

218. Rebekah helped to fool Isaac into believing Jacob was Esau to receive the following:

A) His possessions
B) His blessings
C) Neither A nor B
D) Both A and B

Genesis 27:15–29

219. Since Jacob had stolen his brother's blessing, what blessing did Isaac give Esau?

A) His dwelling would be the fatness of the earth
B) By the sword he would live
C) That he would break his brother's yoke from off his neck
D) All of the above

Genesis 27:37–40

220. Esau plotted to kill his brother, Jacob, for stealing his blessing from their old and blind father. What did Jacob do?

A) He killed Esau first.
B) He fled to Haron.
C) He went to talk with Esau.
D) None of the above

Genesis 27:41–45

221. When did Jacob accept God as Lord of his life?

A) After He appeared in a dream
B) After He told him all He would do for him
C) After He provided him with food and clothes
D) All of the above

Genesis 28:12–21

222. What did Jacob say he would give God because of the many blessings and favor God would give him?

A) He would build God an altar.
B) He would give to the needy.
C) He would give a portion back to God.
D) He would give a tenth of what God gave him.

Genesis 28:22

223. Laban, Rebekah's brother, had two daughters with the following names:

A) Leah and Rachel
B) Dinah and Deborah
C) Sara and Lina
D) None of the above

Genesis 29:16–17

224. Jacob loved Rachel and promised to serve her father, Laban, for the following amount of time to obtain the right to marry Rachel:

A) Seven years
B) Ten years
C) Twelve years
D) Laban gave her willingly.

Genesis 29:17–20

225. After he served seven years for Laban, Jacob took the following woman as his wife:

A) Rachel
B) Leah
C) Dinah
D) Both A and B

Genesis 29:20–26

226. Jacob had to serve Laban for how many more years to obtain the right to marry Rachel:

A) Seven years
B) Ten years
C) Twelve years
D) She was given willingly.

Genesis 29:25–27

Note

In reading Genesis 29 and 30, notice how time after time Jacob was tricked and deceived just as he had tricked his brother, Esau.

227. Jacob took Leah and Rachel to be his wives. Why did God open Leah's womb and not Rachel's?

A) Jacob loved Leah more.
B) Leah was older than Rachel.
C) Jacob hated Leah and loved Rachel.
D) Leah was his wife, and Rachel was not.

Genesis 29:30–31

228. Why did Jacob's anger kindle against Rachel?

A) Rachel blamed Jacob for being barren with no child.
B) Rachel envied her sister.
C) She wanted to die.
D) Both A and C

Genesis 30:1–2

229. When Reuben brought his mother, Leah, mandrakes, what did Rachel say to Leah?

A) "Let me buy some."
B) "Let me have some."
C) She told Reuben to go get her some.
D) She said nothing at all.

Genesis 30:14

230. Leah gave Rachel mandrakes for what reason?

A) So Rachel would be quiet
B) So Rachel would go away
C) So Jacob would go in unto Leah
D) To make Jacob leave Rachel

Genesis 30:14–16

Note

Notice how Leah was in denial the entire time about Jacob ever committing to her (Genesis 30).

231. Jacob and his first wife, Leah, had a daughter. Her name was as follows:

A) Rebekah
B) Dinah
C) Rachel
D) None of the above

Genesis 30:20-21

232. Jacob and his second wife, Rachel, had two sons. The first son's name was as follows:

A) Reuben
B) Simeon
C) Joseph
D) Benjamin

Genesis 30:22–24

233. When the angel of God appeared to Jacob, reminding Jacob of his vow to make God Lord of his life, what did the angel of God tell him to do?

A) Sacrifice his firstborn son
B) Leave his country and family
C) Flee Laban's land and return to Jacob's family's land
D) Get out of Laban's land and go to another one

Genesis 31:11–13

Note

Remember Jacob had fled his country because he stole his brother Esau's birthright. Yet Isaac, their father, had placed a blessing on Esau concerning his brother, Jacob.

234. After Jacob fled Laban's land, what did Laban do?

A) Mourned for the loss of family
B) Pursued Jacob for seven days' journey
C) Got very upset and destroyed the land
D) Nothing

Genesis 31:17–23

235. Laban was upset that Jacob had fled in secret. Who protected Jacob from Laban?

A) Jacob himself
B) The men with Jacob
C) God
D) Rachel

Genesis 31:26–29

Note

Laban did not serve the God of Abraham. Notice that Laban was very upset that his gods had been stolen, so much so he searched every possible area of Jacob's camp for them.

Genesis 31:30–34

236. According to Genesis 31:19, Rachel stole images and small gods from her father, Laban, when he searched her tent. What was she sitting on?

A) The floor
B) A chair
C) Camel furniture
D) A bed

Genesis 31:34

237. Laban did not find his gods when he searched Rachel's tents. Why did she not get up when he requested?

A) She was hiding his gods underneath her.
B) Her menstrual cycle, the custom of women, was upon her.
C) She was not well.
D) Both A and B

Genesis 31:34–35

Note

In certain Bibles there are references to the Nuz, tablets that further express what Laban's dilemma was when he was absent of his gods.

Laban's choice to serve other gods brought on traditions or customs. One custom was that whoever was in possession of the human figure gods was head and ruler of the household.

Think

Laban pursued Jacob for seven days with the expectation of finding his human figure gods, and according to his custom, he would have the legal right to return his family and all his possessions back to his land.

238. Jacob began to argue with Laban. Why?

A) Laban had torn up Jacob's camp, looking for stolen gods.
B) Laban had hotly pursued him.
C) Laban had accused Jacob of stealing but had found nothing in his possession.
D) All of the above

Genesis 31:36–42

239. Before Jacob got to his brother Esau's land, what did Jacob do?

A) Sent messengers ahead
B) Divided his family into separate groups
C) Sent servants with gifts
D) All of the above

Genesis 32:1–19

240. After Jacob had separated from his family in Genesis 32, what happened to his thigh?

A) He cut it.
B) It was out of joint.
C) It became bruised.
D) It got shot.

Genesis 32:24–25

241. Why was Jacob wrestling with a man in Genesis 32?

A) For a blessing
B) For money
C) For protection
D) All of the above

Genesis 32:24–26

Think

Jacob's name was changed to Israel, and Jacob said that he had seen God face-to-face and that his life had been preserved. Who was the man Jacob was wrestling with for his blessing?

Genesis 32:27–30

242. It had been years since Esau had seen Jacob. What happened when they finally met again?

A) They had a battle.
B) Esau killed Jacob.
C) Esau welcomed Jacob and invited him back to his land.
D) The angel of the Lord appeared.

Genesis 33:8–12

243. Dinah, the daughter of Leah and Jacob, was raped by Shechem, the son of Hamor. What else did he want from her?

A) Children
B) To be his wife
C) To be his servant
D) All of the above

Genesis 34:1–4

244. Shechem went to Jacob and asked for Dinah's hand in marriage. What did Jacob require for such a union?

A) All that Shechem had
B) Nothing. He said no.
C) Nothing. He killed him.
D) That all of Hamor's (Shechem's father) males and sons be circumcised

Genesis 34:11–15

245. What was Shechem's consequence for defiling Dinah?

A) Death
B) Favor
C) A union
D) None of the above

Genesis 34:24–27

Note

If any man defile the temple of God, him shall God destroy; for the temple of God is holy, which temple ye are (1 Corinthians 3:17).

246. In Genesis 35 God spoke to Jacob and told him to go to Beth-el. What did Jacob tell his family to do?

A) "Put away the strange gods that are among you."
B) "Be clean."
C) "Change your garments."
D) All of the above

Genesis 35:2–3

247. When Jacob left for Beth-el, what did all his people give him?

A) All the strange gods in their hands
B) All the earrings in their ears
C) Both A and B
D) None of the above

Genesis 35:4–5

Think

Why would the people of Jacob give him all their earrings in their ears when he told them to put away strange gods, be clean, and change their garments? Research earrings to find out the answer.

248. In Genesis 32:28 a man said Jacob's name was changed, and in Genesis 35:10 God said unto Jacob that his name would be changed. What was his name changed to?

A) Ishmael
B) Israel
C) David
D) None of the above

Genesis 35:10–11

249. Jacob and his second wife, Rachel, had two sons; the second son's name was the following:

A) Reuben
B) Simeon
C) Joseph
D) Benjamin

Genesis 35:16–18

250. Jacob (also called Israel by God) had how many sons?

A) Ten
B) Eleven
C) Twelve
D) Thirteen

Genesis 35:21–22

251. Isaac died just like his father, Abraham. How did Isaac die?

A) He was murdered.
B) He gave up the ghost.
C) He was killed in battle.
D) He drowned.

Genesis 35:29

252. Who was Esau the father of?

A) The Edomites
B) The Canaanites
C) The Israelites
D) Both A and C

Genesis 36:43

253. Of the twelve sons of Israel, which son did Jacob love the most, and why?

A) Reuben, because he was the oldest
B) Joseph, because he was born of his old age
C) Benjamin, because he was the youngest
D) None. He loved his daughter, Dinah, more than all the sons.

Genesis 37:3–4

254. Joseph's eleven brothers hated him because he was favored by their father. What did they eventually do to Joseph?

A) They killed him.
B) They left him to die in a well.
C) They sold him into slavery.
D) Both A and B

Genesis 37:26–28

255. Who did Joseph's brothers sell him to?

A) Midianites
B) Ishmaelites
C) Canaanites
D) Edomites

Genesis 37:27–28

256. The brothers of Joseph convinced their father, Israel, that Joseph was dead by doing the following:

A) Bringing back his bloody shoes
B) Bringing back his bloody pants
C) Bringing back his bloody coat
D) All of the above

Genesis 37:31–36

257. There was a man slain because of his wickedness in Genesis. What was his name?

A) Onan
B) Judah
C) Er
D) Beor

Genesis 38:7

258. What did the Lord do to the man, Onan, who spilled child-bearing seed on the ground?

A) Slew him
B) Made him barren
C) Gave him more children than anyone in the Bible
D) Nothing

Genesis 38:7–10

259. Why did Judah want his daughter-in-law burned?

A) She deceived him.
B) She played a harlot and was pregnant with his children.
C) She stole from him.
D) All of the above

Genesis 38:15–18 and 24–27

260. Joseph was sold into slavery to Potiphar (captain of the guard) in the following place:

A) Egypt
B) Canaan
C) Bethel
D) None of the above

Genesis 39:1–2

261. Who was with Joseph when he was bought by Potiphar, captain of the guard for Pharaoh?

A) Other enslaved men
B) His brothers
C) The Lord
D) Angels

Genesis 39:2

262. Why did Joseph find grace in his master's sight?

A) The master needed a supervisor.
B) The Lord made all he did to prosper.
C) The master was getting older.
D) Joseph performed miracles before his master's eyes.

Genesis 39:2–4

263. Who tried to get Joseph to sin against God?

A) Potiphar
B) His master's wife
C) The chief baker
D) Pharaoh

Genesis 39:7–9

264. Joseph was accused of rape by Potiphar's wife. What did Potiphar do about it?

A) He had Joseph's head cut off.
B) He threw him in prison.
C) He chained and beat him.
D) None of the above

Genesis 39:17–22

265. What did Joseph do in prison that ultimately got him out of prison?

A) He dreamed dreams.
B) He had good success.
C) He interpreted dreams.
D) He came up with a way to escape.

Genesis 40:8–14

266. On Pharaoh's birthday, whom did he hang?

A) Joseph
B) His chief baker
C) His wife
D) His chief butler

Genesis 40:20–22

267. Why was Pharaoh's spirit troubled in Genesis 41?

A) Because he hung men to death
B) Because his wife cheated on him
C) Because he had two disturbing dreams with no interpretation
D) All of the above

Genesis 41:1–8

268. Who did Joseph say would give Pharaoh an answer of peace with his dream?

A) Joseph
B) Potiphar
C) God
D) His wife

Genesis 41:15–16

269. What was the reason for Pharaoh having the same dream twice?

A) It was established by God.
B) It would shortly come to pass.
C) He would remember it all.
D) Both A and B

Genesis 41:32

270. Pharaoh put Joseph in the following role:

A) In charge of all of Egypt
B) In the lion's pit
C) In chains in prison
D) None of the above

Genesis 41:37–44

Note

Remember that Joseph had been sold into slavery by his brothers. He also had been rebuked by his father for having a dream that one day they would bow down to the earth in front of him.

Genesis 37:9–10

271. During Egypt's famine, Joseph saw his brothers. What did he accuse them of?

A) Selling him into slavery
B) Being spies
C) Trespassing
D) None of the above

Genesis 42:6–9

272. God foresaw a purpose for Joseph to be sold into slavery in Egypt by his brothers. What was it?

A) To save the people of Egypt
B) To preserve his own people
C) Neither A nor B
D) Both A and B

Genesis 45:4–8

Note

Notice how Joseph acknowledged that it was God's will and plan for him to be sold into slavery and how God used him to preserve life.

Think

See the power that lay within Joseph's hands, given by God. Pharaoh told Joseph's family to come and dwell with them in Egypt and have no regard for their stuff because the good of all the land was theirs.

Genesis 45:17–20

273. God told Jacob, Israel, not to fear going to Egypt, for He would do the following:

A) Allow Joseph to put his hand upon Jacob's eyes
B) Surely bring him up again
C) Make of him a great nation
D) All of the above

Genesis 46:2–4

Note

Notice in Genesis 46 and 47 that through Joseph, not only were his family's lives saved, but their cattle were saved as well. And those who were worthy of being employed got jobs.

Think

In Genesis 46:31–34 Joseph told his brothers to tell Pharaoh they were shepherds. However, this occupation was an abomination unto the Egyptians. Was Pharaoh not an Egyptian? Why would Pharaoh show so much favor toward the shepherds?

Research Pharaoh and see God's work and covering.

274. The famine in Egypt was distressingly severe, and their money failed. What did the Egyptians have to give for food?

A) Land
B) Cattle
C) Themselves
D) All of the above

Genesis 47:12–19

Note

Remember that Joseph's family, who were Hebrews, ruled over Pharaoh's cattle.

275. Who bought all the land for Pharaoh?

A) Joseph
B) The Egyptians
C) The Hebrews
D) Pharaoh

Genesis 47:20

276. What land in Egypt did Pharaoh not buy?

A) Land of Canaan
B) Land of Goshen
C) Land of the priests
D) Land with no water

Genesis 47:22

277. Jacob, Israel, lived in Egypt for seventeen years before he gave up the ghost. Where was he buried?

A) In Egypt
B) In Egypt. Then they moved his remains to his own land.
C) In the cave in the field of Machpelah
D) Abel-mizraim

Genesis 49:28–33

278. After Israel died, his sons feared Joseph. Why?

A) Joseph secretly hated his brothers.
B) Joseph threatened to kill them all upon their father's death.
C) Guilt had set in for what they had done to Joseph.
D) Vengeance was a custom.

Genesis 50:15–17

Note

In Genesis 50:19, Joseph told his brothers to fear not and then told them vengeance was God's, not his. Then he enlightened his brothers' on how their thoughts were evil but God's thoughts were good toward him.

Throughout the Bible, there is countless times where God's favor, grace, mercy, and love prevail over the Enemy concerning those who choose to obey and follow God. Regardless of how bad the situation is, God is always right there to see His children through (Hebrews 13:5–6). God will never leave us nor forsake us.

In the beginning the Enemy prevailed over humankind, and now through Jesus Christ, humankind can prevail over the Enemy.

Think

Q. Why and how can sinners be saved by grace and adopted into God's kingdom through his Son Jesus Christ?

A. There were two classes of beings created (Psalm 8:3–6, Hebrews 2:3–7).

Remember, God gave his only begotten Son to the world, and those children of the world who believed in his Son received adoption into the king- dom of God (Hebrews 2:14–17, John 3:15–18).

What can we then say? "If God be for us, who can be against us?" (Romans 8:31–39)

Note

Note

Printed in the United States
By Bookmasters